T0296700

How to Defeat Advanced Malware
New Tools for Protection and Forensics

How to Defeat Advanced Malware
New Tools for Protection and Forensics

Henry Dalziel

ELSEVIER

AMSTERDAM • BOSTON • HEIDELBERG
LONDON • NEW YORK • OXFORD • PARIS
SAN DIEGO • SAN FRANCISCO
SINGAPORE • SYDNEY • TOKYO

Syngress is an Imprint of Elsevier

SYNGRESS.

Syngress is an imprint of Elsevier
225 Wyman Street, Waltham, MA 02451, USA

British Library Cataloguing-in-Publication Data
A catalogue record for this book is available from the British Library.

Library of Congress Cataloging-in-Publication Data
A catalog record for this book is available from the Library of Congress.

ISBN: 978-0-12-802731-8

For information on all Syngress publications
visit our website at http://store.elsevier.com/

Working together
to grow libraries in
developing countries

www.elsevier.com • www.bookaid.org

TABLE OF CONTENTS

AUTHOR BIOGRAPHY

Henry Dalziel is a serial education entrepreneur, founder of Concise Ac Ltd, online cybersecurity blogger, and e-book author. He writes for the blog "Concise-Courses.com" and has developed numerous cybersecurity continuing education courses and books. Concise Ac Ltd develops and distributes continuing education content (books and courses) for cybersecurity professionals seeking skill enhancement and career advancement. The company was recently accepted onto the UK Trade & Investment's (UKTI) Global Entrepreneur Programme (GEP).

CONTRIBUTING EDITOR BIOGRAPHY

Simon Crosby is cofounder and CTO at Bromium and The Bromium Labs. The Bromium Labs team of security analysts has extensive experience in building innovative technologies to counter and defend against advanced attacks. While Bromium has created an innovative new technology called microvirtualization to address the enterprise security problem and provide protection for end users against advanced malware.

CHAPTER *1*

A Primer on Detection for Security

The security industry has relied for years on endpoint protection software that aims to detect specific behavioral patterns – signatures – of malware in order to protect a system under attack. Most signatures today attempt to capture key behavioral patterns of all variants of a particular exploit or class of malware. In fact, McAfee now reports identifying more than 75,000 unique variants of malware per day, most of which are slight variants on a few successful attacks, on a single vulnerability. If one can accurately capture the pattern, a single signature can deal with many variants. This approach is the key to success: The average ".dat" signature file measures 100 MB in size, and with thousands being added every day (Symantec[1] created more than 10 million unique signatures in 2010), the problem of distributing signatures to endpoints has become severe with the net result that PCs can remain unprotected for a long time.

All detectors must be evaluated for accuracy against four key metrics, namely (for a given sample) the proportion of {True Positive, True Negative, False Positive, False Negative} results that the detector produces. The meaning of these is straightforward:

- *TPF*: The frequency of samples that contained attacks and that was correctly identified
- *TNF*: The frequency of samples that did not contain an attack and was not identified
- *FPF*: The frequency of samples that was incorrectly identified as containing an attack, and
- *FNF*: The frequency of samples that contained a real attack that was not identified.

The ROC curve and the four fractions listed above can be shown graphically as the areas of intersection of two statistical distributions. The distributions plot the value of the detector (e.g., the degree of suspicion

---

[1] Wired Business Media, January 06, 2012 "Symantec Confirms Hackers Accessed Source Code of Two Enterprise Security Products."

of the detector that a particular event is a real attack) for both nonattack traffic and the actual attacks. An example ROC curve is shown below.

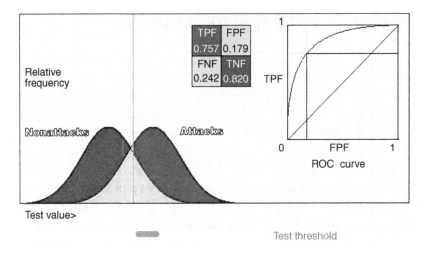

Test value>

Test threshold

Every detector has a threshold at which it will trigger an alarm, and setting the threshold is critical to the utility of the detector in practice. What is the key is the ability of the detector to separate real attacks from normal traffic. A better detector separates the two curves more cleanly, leaving less overlap. The challenge is to accurately detect attacks given the enormous number of slight variations in malware that can be easily generated by an attacker, without increasing the False Positive or False Negative frequencies to the point that the detector is not useful.

It is important to understand that:

1. No detector is perfect. When a detector fails (False Negative), the attacker will succeed.
2. Tuning a detector is a careful balance of trading off False Positives (which train users/IT teams to ignore alarms) against False Negatives (which in turn allow attackers to successfully avoid detection), and doing so requires careful analysis by experts, and a large, relevant data set to check against.
3. Unfortunately today's rapidly moving front of highly tailored malware adapts fast, leaves no time for human assessment, and makes historical attack data sets used to tune detectors significantly less useful.

4. It has been proven that it is impossible to build a useful signature-based detector for polymorphic malware: "The challenge of signature-based detection is to model a space on the order of $O(28n)$ signatures to catch attacks hidden by polymorphism. To cover thirty-byte decoders requires $O(2240)$ potential signatures; for comparison there exist an estimated 280 atoms in the universe."[2]

1.1 TODAY'S APPROACH: "COMPROMISE-FIRST DETECTION"

The endpoint protection industry (EPP) today relies on classic signature-based attack detection. We call this "compromise-first detection" because the increasing difficulty of differentiating between normal and attacker behavior has resulted in both high False Positives and high False Negatives. This occurs when the detector is unable to sufficiently distinguish between attack and non-attack traffic, causing significant overlap of the two distributions measured by the detector, as shown further. The ratio of the TPF to FPF is sometimes called the signal to noise ratio (SNR). A low SNR loses True Positives in a sea of False Positives, training users, and administrators to ignore warnings, and wasting the time of security staff.

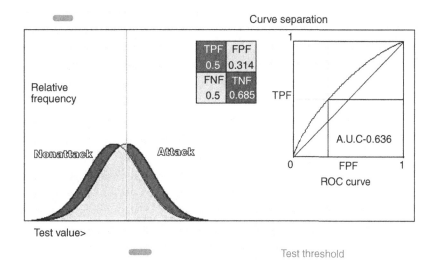

[2] On the Infeasibility of Modeling Polymorphic Shellcode, Columbia University.

As a result, the EPP industry has come to rely heavily on detectors that are sufficiently accurate only if they detect malware when it actually compromises the system, for example, when it overwrites a key Windows system dynamic-link library (DLL) or registry entry, or persists a file with a known-bad signature. Unfortunately, at this point, the system has already been compromised and must at the very least be reimaged, incurring costs to IT and downtime for users. Worse still, sophisticated attacks are crafted to immediately take advantage of an exploit, so with this type of detection, by the time the alert has been raised or blocking initiated (such as terminating a connection), the attacker may already have achieved his/her goal, such as stealing a file or moving deeper into the enterprise infrastructure. From the moment an attacker first compromises a single machine, the cost of remediation increases exponentially with time, because the attacker will rapidly penetrate deeper into the enterprise, causing more damage, requiring substantial additional remediation, and exposing more users and data.

Compromise-first detection is problematic. Delays in signature distribution together with detector inaccuracy aid the attacker, and the cost of remediation is high – all systems that might have been penetrated must be reimaged.

Ultimately, EPP vendors face an impossible challenge trading off False Positives versus False Negatives: They lose either way, and so do their customers.

CHAPTER 2

2014 Endpoint Exploitation Trends

Before analyzing potential solutions, security teams tasked with protecting critical enterprise assets must track the shifting attack landscape to understand key attack methods and targets. The Author, in conjunction with Bromium Labs, a team of security analysts with extensive experience in building innovative technologies to counter and defend against advanced attacks, studied key trends in the 2014 cyber-attack landscape. These latest trends are summarized below and should be factored into security planning in the coming months:

1. Microsoft® Internet Explorer set a record high for reported vulnerabilities in the first half of 2014.
2. Microsoft Internet Explorer also leads in publicly reported exploits.
3. Web browser release cycles are becoming more frequent – as are initial security patches.
4. Adobe Flash is the primary browser plugin being targeted by 2014 zero-day attacks.
5. New "Action Script Spray" techniques targeting Flash have been uncovered that exploit zero-day vulnerabilities.

2.1 ZERO-DAY TRENDS

In the first half of 2014, the growth in zero-day exploitation continued unabated from 2013. Unsurprisingly, all of the zero-day attacks targeted end-user applications such as browsers and applications such as Microsoft® Office. Typically these attacks were launched using classic spear-phishing tactics. Although Microsoft Internet Explorer was the most patched product on the market, it was also the most exploited, surpassing Oracle Java and Adobe Flash. Bromium Labs believes that Microsoft Internet Explorer will likely continue to be the target of choice going forward.

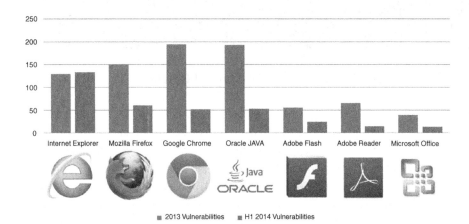

Source: NVD.

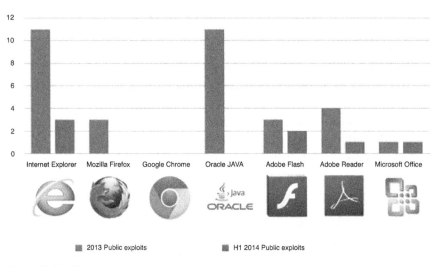

Source: Exploit-db.com.

In comparison, Java had no reported zero-day exploitation in the first half of 2014.

Released in late 2013, Microsoft Internet Explorer 11 has seen a quick succession of security patches, compared to its predecessors. Bromium Labs analyzed the timelines for each Internet Explorer patch release and documented when the first critical patch became Generally Available (GA).

Internet Explorer release to patch timeline.

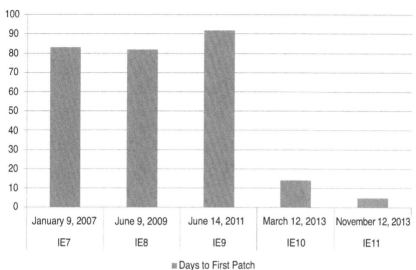

Days to First Patch

	January 9, 2007	June 9, 2009	June 14, 2011	March 12, 2013	November 12, 2013
	IE7	IE8	IE9	IE10	IE11

■ Days to First Patch

2.2 NOTABLE ZERO-DAY EXPLOITATION TECHNIQUES

Microsoft Internet Explorer

- Almost all Microsoft Internet Explorer memory corruption exploits now use de facto ROP (Return Oriented Programming) techniques for bypassing the default operating system security mechanisms (address space layout randomization (ASLR), data execution prevention (DEP)).
- Both the Microsoft Internet Explorer zero-day exploits leveraged "Action Script Spray" technique to bypass ASLR.

Adobe Flash

- Attackers were quick to leverage new features released in late 2013 to exploit ActionScript Virtual Machine ASVM implementation flaws using "Action Script Spray" techniques.
- Non-ASLR libraries continued to be the weakest link leveraged by malware authors to bypass OS protections.

Adobe Reader Sandbox Escape

- This vulnerability was uncovered late in 2013 and was finally patched in January 2014.

- Two vulnerabilities were used to bypass the Adobe Reader sandbox:
  - o CVE-2013-3346: Use-after-free vulnerability in Adobe Reader
  - o CVE-2013-5065: Kernel-mode zero day vulnerability NDProxy.sys

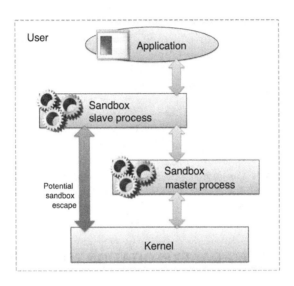

Adobe Flash Player and Recent Client Exploits

2010–2013 were clearly the years of Java exploits. Since then, a lot has changed: old versions of JRE are blocked by default, Java applets now require explicit activation from users resulting in this attack vector becoming harder to leverage. In response to increased defense deployed by security vendors and software developers, attackers have switched to new plugins. In the past 6 months, Adobe Flash Player was seen to be abused leveraging two attack vectors:

- Exploiting ASVM vulnerabilities
- Abetting exploitation of IE UAF bugs

2.3 EMERGING ZERO-DAY EXPLOITATION TECHNIQUES

Action Script Virtual Machine Attacks

In 2014, there were three severe vulnerabilities that were detected in live attacks. Unlike Java, where in the main, malicious code leveraged JRE's capabilities, Flash exploits require DEP and ASLR bypass for successful execution. The following table provides a summary of 2014 ASVM attacks.

CVE	Vulnerability	Exploitation Technique
2014-0497	N/A	Non-ASLR libraries of Flash Player
2014-0502	Double Free of AS3 Shared Object	Non-ASLR libraries of JRE 1.6 and 1.7 and MS Office 2007 and 2010, ROP chain is built relative to fixed offset
2014-0515	Heap overflow in compiled Shader	Dynamic ROP generation based on Action Script Spray

Unlike the first two exploits, CVE-2014-0515 used a relatively new technique to bypass ASLR allowing dynamic crafting of ROP chain called Action Script Spray. This technique was also seen in two IE exploits released in 2014.

ROP Bypass Using Action Script Spray

Both IE exploits released in 2014 (CVE-2014-1776, CVE-2014-0322) used Flash to build the ROP chain and launch shellcode. This technique leverages the way dense arrays are allocated in the endpoints memory.

If a vulnerability allows an attacker to control the size of a vector they could make it as big as the whole memory space and then search for the necessary API calls and ROP gadgets. The following picture illustrates an Action Script Spray attack.

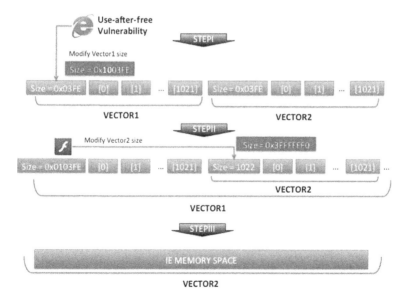

If the whole process memory is accessible, an attacker can now craft an ROP chain using ASVM capabilities and modify vtable with a pointer to the shellcode and trigger it.

The attack is more complex than a traditional heap spray, which indicates that cybercriminals are ready to invest more time and resources into development of new techniques in response to ever increasing protection measures. In addition to that, the prevalence of IE + Flash is much higher than IE + Java JRE, so this has provided attackers with a larger opportunity.

CHAPTER 3

The Proposed Solution

Computing has changed dramatically over the past decade. Even the most prophetic among us could not have foreseen how cloud computing was going to shift and "even out" the playing field, specifically as it relates to computer storage and networking. Pay-as-you-go cloud infrastructure for application developers and affordable, powerful, touch-enabled mobile devices have transformed client computing forever.

The future of computing continues to be reshaped by powerful forces: cloud-based applications continue to grow in popularity, accessed in the main by personally owned mobile telephones, tablets and computers, via an inherently unsafe internet. And as a result, operating systems, networks, and applications will continue to be susceptible to attack, and although we can expect this challenge to be met head-on by cloud service providers, clearly the sheer scale of the bring your own device (BYOD) phenomenon would indicate that the same cannot be said for client devices. So it stands to reason that computer systems must defend themselves "by design." Significant infrastructural and trust-related changes are needed in this "cloud-mobile" era. Defense must be an intrinsic element of computer system design.

At the heart of this issue is "Trustworthy Computing."[1] Our goal is to propose a new systems architecture solution that not only answers the security needs of future systems, to combat, for example, the zero-day exploits outlined above, but more importantly, a system architecture that deals with our existing "leaky" end-point legacy systems (which continue to be the front line), and offer up the most vulnerable operating systems and applications to attack. Although the concepts we discuss could also be applied to server-class systems, our main focus here is on client devices.

---

[1] Wikipedia, "Trustworthy Computing" [Online]

3.1 THE PRINCIPLE OF LEAST PRIVILEGE

Humans are inherently social, and our notion of trust is innate. In fact, trust has always been closely associated to survival. We routinely limit the amount of information that we share with others on the basis of what we feel they needs to know. Information, if one were to apply a digital analogy, is shared on a "policy of least privilege."

Although we can understand this instinctively, one of the inherent challenges in cyber security is accommodating the fact that humans also expect their computer systems to have the same ability, to switch between trust domains, and decide what information should be shared, how it should be shared, and what level of access somebody should have to it. We see no issue with using the same mobile device to chat via Twitter, for example, whereas moments later, check our personal bank balances. Phishing attacks continue to grow in popularity, and the consequences of an uninformed user clicking what looks to be a legitimate link in an e-mail, only to see their action invite malware that attacks vulnerability in an operating system, are all too familiar.

The challenge security teams face is both to protect their networks and simultaneously allow their employees to leverage the productivity benefits afforded by, for example, social media and cloud-based applications.

This reality is further complicated by the very business model the "free" Internet has been built around. Online advertising companies and search engines benefit from compromised security. For example, many sites require personal information from users, and make money by selling that information to marketing firms and vendors. A user may be persuaded that a site will respect the user's right to privacy, even when the implicit exchange is free service for the right to sell your data.

That instinctive ability to determine the level of privilege somebody should have in a social relationship is dependent upon "granularity." Unfortunately, today's operating systems (OSes) and applications (e.g., web browsers) are incapable of providing either a similar degree of granularity, or effective embodiment of trust domains, or confinement to apply the concept of least privilege. Critical OS design concepts come from a pre-internet age, where designers did not have to take into account targeted attacks that exploit unpatched weaknesses within the operating system or software, or deliberate monitoring systems that jeopardize individual privacy.

Although all operating systems utilize some kind of software isolation (e.g., sandboxing), access controls, and hardware defense (e.g., user and kernel modes) to segment applications, OS services and data, with the objective of applying least privilege, they cannot manage their inherent, latent vulnerability.

Operating systems offer hackers an enormous attack surface (e.g., the Windows operating system and Android mobile operating systems have approximately 50,000,000 and 10,000,000 lines of code respectively[2]). Mobile device market differentiation boils down to a constantly growing feature list, but it is exactly those features that expose the consumers mobile device to vulnerabilities – approximately 1 significant defect/KLOC that can allow an attacker to increase execution rights and compromise the computer to get into both local and remote resources.[3]

Consumers are also susceptible to the existence of applications that allow websites and search engines to monitor their behavior and betray privacy. Often these applications (e.g., Google Chrome) come from companies whose very aim is to profit from their monitoring of consumers, while apparently offering value (functionality, or claims of security) within their applications. Although privacy is a sophisticated subject that requires an extensive attention on its own, it likewise utilizes a solid implementation of least privilege. Both security and privacy necessitate that our computers are trustworthy.

3.2 DETECTION'S FOLLY

Even if the battle between attackers and security vendors is heavily weighted in the attackers favor, the $70 BN cyber security industry hinges its livelihood on identifying malicious behavior. It is our contributing editor's belief (Bromium Labs), however, that this premise is not only flawed, but mathematically impossible.[4] Simply put, vendors will never be able to reliably detect polymorphic malware in order to block it.

---

[2] Wikipedia, "Source Lines of Code"
[3] C. Perrin, "The danger of complexity: more code, more bugs," TechRepublic
[4] Wikipedia, "The Halting Problem"

We must recognize that, much like us, our computer systems cannot efficiently differentiate good from bad. Antivirus and other security products that boast of being capable of detecting malware, put simply, cannot keep up to date. In reality, detection rates for today's advanced threats are generally around 5–10%.

CHAPTER *4*

Protection's Weak Link

In response, an array of defensive security technologies has been developed that aims to complement traditional detection-centric approaches. They include antivirus systems, host intrusion prevention systems, desktop firewalls, desktop virtualization systems, patch management solutions, and application whitelisting solutions. Before we continue, it is worth reviewing these solutions before introducing what we believe to be the cyber-security panacea.

Antivirus (AV) systems detect malware by using signatures that are developed from samples of attacks that have successfully compromised other users. The addition of heuristics and cloud-based lookups has decreased the time needed for AV systems to detect known attacks, but with over 3 billion unique pieces of malware discovered in 2011 alone, today's attackers have little problem avoiding these systems.

Host intrusion prevention systems (IPS) attempt to detect and block malicious attacks by comparing the behavior of vulnerable applications with a pattern that could indicate "malicious behavior." The shortcomings of this technology are that malicious and benign code can perform the same types of operations within an endpoint, and singling out the behavior of a single piece of software can be challenging. A host IPS system that is tuned to be effective against unknown malware will also block many unknown but benign software functions leading to user dissatisfaction and an avalanche of corporate help-desk calls. Host IPS is often disabled or tuned to the point that malware is no longer blocked in reaction to these problems.

Desktop firewalls protect the host system by blocking low-level network requests to specific processes within the endpoint. Desktop firewalls do not provide any protection for the most risky applications like the web browser or opening files and attachments, as these processes must be able to communicate with the outside world to function.

Application whitelisting solutions restrict end users from using "non-approved" programs on their systems. This approach typically has a large impact on user productivity that often results in users finding "work-arounds" such as performing critical tasks on mobile or home products. Application whitelists provide no protection from attacks targeted at the "approved" program level which remain vulnerable to zero-day or targeted attacks routinely delivered within the content the applications are tasked with processing.

Patch management solutions attempt to address the root cause of security exploits by providing fixes or "patches" to the underlying vulnerabilities in the programs that are at risk. Unfortunately the sheer scale and attack surface of today's operating systems and application suites provides endless vulnerabilities. Organizations spend huge amounts of time and money testing and deploying patches in an endless attempt to keep their systems secure with little impact on the number or frequency of successful attacks.

Although adding layers of security to the endpoint is intuitively appealing, it has downsides: It negatively impacts user experience, and more importantly, the security chain is only as strong as its weakest link – the OS kernel. All threat detection/prevention tools depend on the continued integrity of the kernel and are easy to bypass if the kernel can be compromised via a novel exploit – for example, a zero day. Unfortunately critical vulnerabilities in OS kernels are being discovered at an alarming rate.

4.1 DESKTOP VIRTUALIZATION DOES NOT SECURE THE ENDPOINT

In recent years, the growth of desktop virtualization has led to new challenges in endpoint protection. Agents that are deployed on physical Windows desktops do not function well in virtual desktops hosted on a hypervisor. Endpoint Protection Platform (EPP) suites are disk I/O heavy, and on a server running scores of VMs, this leads to collapse of the storage infrastructure and low VM/server density. As a result, each of the major vendors has had to rearchitect its EPP suite for virtualized environments. More importantly, however, it has led to the realization that the virtual infrastructure vendor has a key role to play in endpoint protection, since only the hypervisor has absolute control over all system resources: CPU, memory, storage, and network I/O, for all guests on the system.

Since all products for virtualized environments are in their earliest stages of development, the security of mission critical workloads or virtual desktops on virtual infrastructure is weak, since every compromise that is possible on a physical desktop can be achieved on a virtual one. Of note is a recent NIST study[1] in the area of security for fully virtualized workloads, which notes: "Migrating computing resources to a virtualized environment has little or no effect on most of the resources' vulnerabilities and threats."

Virtualization technology, however, will be the key to the delivery of the next generation of security, since a hypervisor can provide a new (more secure) locus of execution for security software. The hypervisor has control over all system resources (CPU, memory, and all I/O) and is intimately involved in the execution of all guest VMs, giving it an unparalleled view of system state and a unique opportunity to provide powerful insights into the security of the system overall. Since the hypervisor relies on a much smaller code base than a full OS, it also has a much smaller attack surface. Finally, it has an opportunity to contain malware that does successfully penetrate a guest, within the VM container. Ultimately, the hypervisor provides a new, highly privileged runtime environment with an opportunity to provide greater control over endpoint security. Bromium is the only vendor to specifically exploit virtualization to both protect endpoints and detect new attacks.

4.2 DETECTION AND ISOLATION USING VMs

Many security vendors have attempted to use virtual machines as sacrificial run-time instances or "honeypots." Traffic entering the system (an endpoint or a network) is first directed to a sacrificial VM containing the operating system and its applications. Although it is attractive, this approach has drawbacks: It relies on an attack occurring, and being detected in the honeypot before the traffic is passed on to its intended recipient. But most malware can detect that it is running in a virtualized environment, and modify its behavior to avoid detection.

---

[1] Guide to Security for Full Virtualization Technologies, National Institute of Standards and Technology.

A degenerate form of this approach relies on isolating an entire application, such as a web browser, in a VM to contain attacks. However, application performance suffers, and the approach lacks granularity: A successful but undetected attack from a single site can compromise all subsequent browser tabs and sites visited, including those that access trusted intranet and SaaS applications.

CHAPTER 5

Micro-Virtualization

Micro-virtualization is a new system architecture that uses hardware-virtualization features, as offered on current CPUs, along with an innovative hypervisor called a Microvisor, to effortlessly hardware-isolate user-initiated activities or software programs operating on an endpoint. Hardware-isolated activities (called micro-VMs) are given a virtualized file system and network stack whose access privileges are contained in accordance to the principles of least privilege: The task has access only to the specific file(s), IP services, websites, and subnets which it needs, and no more. In addition, the task has no access to system hardware or any other privileged system resource.

Micro-virtualization applies granular hardware isolation of individual activities to robustly impose least privilege, access to privileged resources (e.g., networks, devices, and the file system) takes place through a narrow hypercall interface.[1] If a task is compromised, malware will be safely contained by the virtualization hardware which ensures CPU, memory, and I/O isolation. To endanger the Microvisor, malware must attack the computer via the hypercall interface that is applied in approximately 10 KLOC and thoroughly hardened. The Microvisor makes sure mandatory access control for access to any privileged system resources to prevent privilege escalation, and it also immediately converts the format of harmful content that accesses privileged resources (printers, clipboard, etc.) to stop potentially harmful content from striking the OS kernel.

Micro-virtualization offers numerous benefits:

- The Microvisor can be utilized on all modern CPU architectures, and can be stacked on a conventional hypervisor. Bromium's application uses an extension of the open-source Xen Hypervisor[2] called micro-Xen[3] that runs on x86 and ARM platforms that

---

[1] The Linux Foundation, "Hypercall"
[2] The Linux Foundation, "The Xen Project"
[3] I. Pratt, "Micro-Xen," Bromium Inc, September 2012

support hardware virtualization. It has a small code base – about half the size of Xen – making it easier to harden.

- The Microvisor is a late-load hypervisor that is distributed to PC/laptop endpoints as with any program. It may also be simply incorporated by system manufacturers on tablet and mobile phone systems, without the need to modify the operating system.
- Micro-VMs are usually light-weight hardware isolation containers that, unlike VMs, can be created and destroyed quickly (about 10ms), so that they can be applied at the granularity of a single user task (e.g., each tab in the browser) and with negligible effect on the user experience.
- Micro-VMs execute copy-on-write (CoW). All changes to memory space or files are separated in a throw-away cache that is removed when the task ends, making the system organically self-remediating.
- Finally, the granular makeup of a micro-VM facilitates per-task introspection, simplifying the identification and forensic monitoring of malware as it runs in isolation.

5.1 RELATED WORK

Despite the fact that mainstream OSes that take time and effort to secure computer systems, such as the CAP[4] and Multics,[5] have already been built. However, their inherent benefits have not been widely adopted. This reality is most likely just as much a consequence of market expediencies (the growth of DOS to Windows, and thence NT; and the horizontal nature of the computer marketplace); and to the complexity that security normally imposes on systems management and end users. For example, Windows User Account Control (introduced in Vista) alerts an individual anytime he/she opens an "untrusted" file downloaded from the web, or an attachment. Continued alerts for low-risk events have the same outcome as conventional false positives, that is, teaching an individual to disregard them. Outsourcing security-related responsibilities to the consumer result in lowered security, as users go around the bad user experience.

---

[4] Wikipedia, "CAP computer"
[5] T. Van Vleck, "Multics"

What we need is a technology designed for granular isolation of trust domains that will be easily implemented and controlled at scale – including on legacy systems, which increases system security, and reduces the impact on end user experience.

Isolation technologies abound:

- Classical OS structure utilizes isolation through separation of untrustworthy user processes from the system kernel, and recent studies have concentrated on boosting OS design[6,7]
- Sandboxes effort to retrofit software-based isolation between user space application processes and existing insecure operating system kernels, using software programs.
- The use of a hypervisor and virtualization has been successfully used as an isolation strategy to increase system security, for example, in the Xbox 360[8] and in a variety of embedded systems.[9]
- Hypervisor-based isolation has been utilized to construct multilevel secure systems, using virtualization to be sure the needed separation of different run-time environments.[10]
- For both client and server class systems, multiple independent operating system instances in VMs can be mutually isolated by a hypervisor; in the client context, this is often presented in the context of desktop virtualization[11] where user interacts with numerous remotely executing desktop VMs whose output is delivered to an endpoint via a remote desktop protocol.[12]
- Other static isolation approaches have been proposed, for example, the Qubes OS[13] in which each application runs in its own VM,

---

[6] Gordon College, Computer Science Department, "Operating System Organization (CPS312)," 2014.
[7] J. N. Herder, H. Bos, B. Gras, P. Homburg and A. S. Tanenbaum, "Isolating Operating System Extensions in User-mode Processes," Computer Science Dept., Vrije Universiteit, Amsterdam, The Netherlands, 2008.
[8] J. Lees, "The hypervisor and its implications" Joystiq
[9] D. K. a. M. Kleidermacher, "Embedded Systems Security - Part 3: Hypervisors and system virtualization," February 2013.
[10] Intel Corporation, "SecureView Delivers More Security, Performance, and Savings"
[11] Wikipedia, "Desktop virtualization"
[12] Microsoft Corporation, "Microsoft Remote Desktop Services (RDS) Explained"
[13] The Invisible Things Lab, "Qubes OS"

Microsoft's Drawbridge[14] which bundles a "library OS" with the application when it is created – similar to the open-source Docker project.[15]

We should examine these kinds of methods against our requirements: user empowerment, system security, and ease of deployment and management at scale. For example:

- On legacy systems, sandboxing is a proven strategy that is simple to set up as an application component, but has been demonstrated to be unsuccessful against a motivated enemy. The well-designed sandboxes of contemporary OSes (including iOS and Windows 8) are significantly better. However, sandboxing the entire application is not adequately granular as a construct for applications (e.g., Word or a browser) that process content from various trust domains. Finally, no sandbox can safeguard against a kernel-level weakness in the OS upon which it runs.
- A hypervisor delivers powerful inter-VM (inter-OS) isolation on a single device, but cannot safeguard code inside a VM itself (e.g., a virtual desktop) from assault. Moreover, implementing and operating a hypervisor as well as the endpoint OS image(s) and applications is onerous. It can also be impractical for end users because it affects the user experience.

Task-centric isolation

We define a trust domain based on the concept of a user-initiated task: all processing (both user and kernel mode) for a user-initiated workflow related to any application content (e.g., a document), or remote web service represents a task (e.g., each email attachment and each top-level domain (TLD) on the web is an independent task.) We achieve this definition through rigorous application of the principle of least privilege, which also allows us to reason about the security and privacy of the entire system, assuming that any task is compromised.

We seek to granularly and mutually isolate (according to least privilege) the execution of many trust domains on a single device,

---

[14] Microsoft Corporation, "Drawbridge"
[15] Docker, Inc., "What is Docker?"

preserving contextual concurrency for the user, and securely permitting interdomain communication and sharing subject to privacy constraints (and in an enterprise context, protection policies).

We aim to ensure that information exposed and therefore vulnerable to theft is minimized:

- An attacker who successfully elevates his/her privileges in the OS context of a single micro-VM must be unable to access any other micro-VM or the host OS.
- The files and other configuration data (such as the Windows SAM and Registry[16]) available to a micro-VM are only those that it specifically needs to execute correctly. For example:
  - The only files needed to render a website are its cookie and DOM storage.
  - When a user is accessing a document, only the document itself is needed.
- Network services, sites, and networks available to a micro-VM are narrowed according to the privilege level of the task. For example:
  - Remote sites and networks of value (e.g., corporate SaaS sites, the user's bank, or a corporate intranet) should not be accessible from a task that only needs access to the untrusted web.
  - High-value network infrastructure services such as a corporate DNS or a VPN should only be accessible to a task that requires access to them.
- No micro-VM is given access to privileged system services (clipboard, printers, devices, access to the display, or user input) without specific need, and then only under-user control and subject to additional safety controls that are explained as follows.
- A task may retain files that survive after the task is terminated, but they must be securely tagged with metadata that stores the trust domain of the task. For example:
  - An isolated web site for TLD A might save a cookie, DOM storage, and a cache of its pages. These may be persisted, but only ever accessed by another isolated renderer for the same TLD A.

---

[16] Wikipedia, "Security Accounts Manager"

- The user might edit an untrusted, isolated Word document B. She/he can save changes to the document that will be stored in the file system together with metadata that records its provenance. The document can only ever be accessed again from another hardware-isolated Word instance with rights to access a document of that provenance.
- Upon termination, all execution state (both kernel- and user-mode memory, and all execution related changes to files) are discarded, eliminating any malware.

5.2 A PRACTICAL EXAMPLE

Least privilege dictates the minimum set of system resources (network, file system, desktop) that a given task needs to function correctly, for example, in the context of the browser, a task is an application context defined by the top-level domain (the site top-level domain). What resources does Facebook.com, for example, really need? It needs its cookie and DOM storage, and access to the untrusted web. If the browser tab for Facebook.com is compromised (e.g., it delivers a poisoned advertisement), we can tolerate loss of the cookie (which compromises user privacy, but not system security). We can live with the fact that malware will have access to the untrusted internet. The system will still be safe if malware cannot:

- see any user keystrokes, mouse input, or gain access to the screen (to copy pixels from the display, or display any content to the user),
- access any other privileged data, for example, files other than the Facebook cookie, or registry entries that might leak valuable information
- gain access to valuable networks or sites (e.g., SaaS sites or the intranet),
- access any privileged devices (printers, webcam, the OS file system, or shares)

Least privilege dictates that the task must not have access to any other resources unless they are explicitly required, and then only under precise control, and only for the shortest possible duration. For example:

- If the user wants to upload a photo to Facebook, he/she can select the photo (in the usual way) on the desktop, and then (only) the selected file will be injected into the hardware-isolated task that is rendering the Facebook.com browser tab.

- If the user wants to download a file, it can be allowed to persist outside the confines of the isolated task, but only if we remember the fact that it is untrusted, so that it can only ever be opened in another hardware-isolated task.

5.3 HARDWARE-ENFORCED TASK ISOLATION

Hardware isolation of tasks is a core tenet because it offers the most robust barrier to attack. Moreover, it allows isolation of both user-mode and kernel mode execution for a user task, protecting the system from exploits that target the OS kernel directly. Specifically, although sand-boxing is becoming popular in many applications, "security by design" vendors aim to bolster system-wide security by extending isolation prop-erties to include kernel processing on behalf of the application. This is crucial because it is often easy to bypass a sandbox by compromising the kernel directly.

5.4 HARDWARE VIRTUALIZATION TECHNOLOGY

In the early years of x86 virtualization, the device hardware was virtual-ized entirely in software, either by patching the binaries of guest VMs, or through a technique known as enlightenment, pioneered in Xen, and adopted in Microsoft Hyper-V.

Over the last few years Intel, AMD, and ARM have introduced hard-ware extensions to their CPUs and chipsets that accelerate and auto-mate many low-level virtualization tasks and assist the hypervisor or Virtual Machine Manager (VMM) with dynamic control over hardware resources and increase the security of the hypervisor and the isolation between VMs. Hardware virtualization support today includes functions that virtualize the CPU, memory (including nested page tables), the I/O subsystem, and networking. Hardware virtualization for GPUs is in its infancy, but is expected to become more widely available as use cases for virtualized graphics become more prevalent. Peripheral interfaces, such as USB, can be easily virtualized in software.

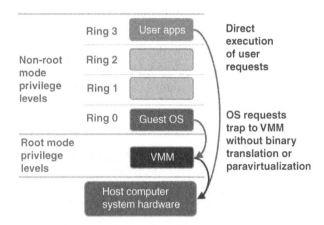

Both Intel and AMD support device I/O virtualization and assignment (Intel VT-d, AMD IOMMU) that permits I/O devices to be safely directly assigned to guest VMs, and protects the hypervisor and other guests from device DMA into system memory. Memory used for device I/O is only visible to the guest that owns the device.

In addition, both Intel TXT and AMD SKINIT offer CPU extensions to permit secure system bootstrap and hardware-based attestation using a Trusted Platform Module (TPM) that securely stores signatures for whitelisted code (such as the hypervisor). In a measured boot, the hardware verifies that the hypervisor has not been modified, and the hypervisor can then in turn check that each guest VM is unmodified, prior to it being started. This permits IT to ensure that the system is in the intended state when booted.

Hardware virtualization has played a crucial role in the broad adoption of virtualization. Without hardware guarantees of isolation between guest VMs and between guests and the hypervisor, it would be difficult to adopt virtual infrastructure for mission critical applications, or to comply with regulations that mandate infrastructure isolation, for example, those of the Payment Card Industry (PCI).

5.5 MICRO-VIRTUALIZATION AT WORK

Micro-virtualization is a second-generation virtualization technology that extends the isolation, control, and security principles of hypervisor-based virtualization into the OS and its applications. It does this by using hardware virtualization to dynamically isolate user tasks.

5.6 THE MICROVISOR

A traditional hypervisor hosts multiple independent guest VMs (each of which executes against a virtual hardware abstraction, and is an independent OS Environment), whereas the Microvisor is a specialized, light-weight, late-load hypervisor that uses hardware virtualization to isolate tasks in Micro-VMs. Unlike traditional VMs, micro-VMs have no virtual hardware interface, they do not boot, cannot be paused, saved, suspended, resumed, moved, or taken snapshot of; they do not have an identity different from the desktop OS, and are temporally dependent on it (they cannot survive a reboot of the host). They are simply user-mode OS tasks that run hardware isolated from the Windows desktop – the OS schedules them for execution, and manages their performance and resource usage.

A traditional VM is "enlightened" with virtualized hardware abstractions (via device drivers for virtual hardware), whereas a micro-VM is enlightened using standard OS mechanisms at the file system and network layer. In addition, all access to the device (graphics, keyboard, mouse, and printing) is virtualized using a virtual access protocol. Each micro-VM renders into local memory, which is securely delivered to the desktop where the user experience is composited. Micro-VMs have no access to USB or other hardware devices.

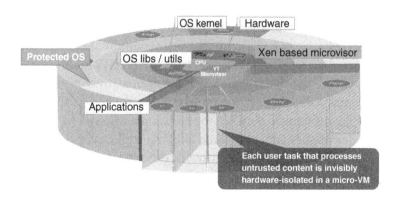

The minimalist approach of micro-virtualization offers many advantages over traditional hypervisor-based and VM-centric virtualization:

- The Microvisor does not have hardware or device driver dependencies.
- It can rely on the OS for task scheduling and device and power management.
- As a result, it can easily be deployed like a typical application to any endpoint that supports hardware virtualization and managed at scale using existing tools and skill-sets
- Finally, the task-centric nature of micro-virtualization permits an unchanged user experience.

Applications installed by the device, vendor, or enterprise IT, run unchanged, but any application tasks that process content from untrusted domains are hardware isolated from the privileged (and protected) host OS. A hardware isolated task in a micro-VM will take a hardware trap (VM_EXIT) in order to request access to any privileged system service, including network access, file system read/write, copy/paste, input/output events and all device access.

When a micro-VM is created, its only way to access these system resources is via "enlightened" service APIs, which use standard OS interface hooks to direct execution control. Whenever the isolated task attempts to access any of these resources the enlightened service, API invokes a hypercall, which in turn causes the virtualization hardware to force a CPU VM_EXIT, suspending execution and permitting the Microvisor to arbitrate access using a set of resource-access-control policies for the task that are both task and trust/privilege-level specific. The Microvisor implements mandatory access control for access to any system resource (e.g., can the user print an untrusted file?) and also manages any data format changes between privilege domains (e.g., when printing a PDF, the document will be converted to a nonthreatening format such as XPS before being transferred to the host, and then to the printer). Files exchanged between the host and a Micro-VM via a simple shared folder mechanism, and all networking traffic is transferred using a hardened, efficient interdomain transport between a micro-VM and the Microvisor, called Xen v4v.

5.7 MEMORY AND CPU ISOLATION

When a micro-VM is created, its memory map contains entries to the OS kernel, libraries, task-specific code, and state. However, when the task executes, all memory access is "Copy on Write" or CoW – any changes the task makes to memory (both user and kernel space) are to a separate, local copy stored in hardware-isolated memory, and not to the original. Notably, if the task is compromised by malware that modifies the kernel or user-space libraries, the malware will only succeed in modifying a locally cached difference against the original, and not the running host.

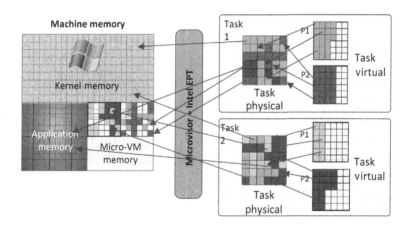

5.8 VIRTUALIZED FILE SYSTEM (VFS)

Each micro-VM is presented with a virtualized file system (VFS) abstraction that provides a view of a golden OS installation and OS configuration state, and a dramatically reduced user file system that contains only the files needed for correct execution of the task. These are determined through application of the "principle of least privilege." Files that need to persist beyond the lifetime of a single task are tagged with metadata that preserves their provenance and untrusted nature. Untrusted files can only be accessed by a micro-VM with the appropriate privilege. For example:

- For a browser renderer (e.g., Internet Explorer, Chrome, or Firefox), the files required include the cookie for the relevant TLD, its DOM storage, and browser cache. These files are also the only files that a browser task can modify and persist.

- For a Multi-Purpose Internet Mail Extensions (MIME)-type handler for a particular untrusted file type, the only file required is the untrusted file itself. This can be persisted beyond the lifetime of the application (e.g., across editing sessions) as an untrusted file.

The virtualized file system implements CoW semantics for any modifications to files, with CoW differences saved at the block level in hardware-isolated memory, for performance and security reasons. So, if malware modifies a file, the Microvisor stores in-memory cached differences between the file and the original (a logical copy) that efficiently records only block deltas against the original. The actual file in the host file system is unchanged.

If a micro-VM needs to save a file (e.g., the user downloads a file in the browser and wishes to save it), the file is securely passed from the micro-VM via the VFS to a user-selected location on the host OS, with metadata tags indicating lack of trust. The user experience is unchanged. Similarly, any file that the user wishes to inject into a micro-VM (e.g., attach a file to a web-mail) is passed via the VFS. Rich policies can be applied to file export from a micro-VM or import into a micro-VM to ensure data-loss prevention and to otherwise control user workflow.

When the micro-VM exits (the user closes the application, the task terminates or the Microvisor terminates the task), the Microvisor discards the task's memory image and uses a persistence policy to determine what modified, task-relevant file-system state is persisted. For example, a browser renderer is permitted to modify and save cookie state, DOM storage, and its own cache.

5.9 VIRTUALIZED IP NETWORKING – THE MOBILE SDN

The Microvisor also restricts micro-VM access to networks and networked services, ensuring that least privilege applies not only locally but also to enforce access control, security, and privacy policy to remote networks and sites accessible from the device. To achieve this it virtualizes all access to IP networking services for each micro-VM. The virtualized network service (VNS) is in many respects a client-side analog of cloud-and-data-center Software Defined Networking (SDN) used to enforce network isolation, security, and privacy per tenant or hosted VM, and provides powerful application-layer control over all network activity.

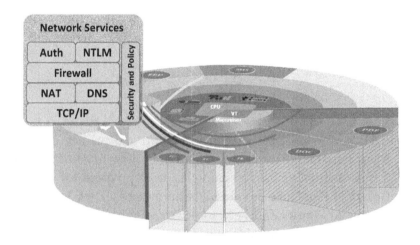

The Microvisor implements the virtualized network service stack in user mode on the device host OS. If the task in a micro-VM attempts to use the network, a CPU enforced VM_EXIT hands control to the Microvisor that enforces security constraints before delegating processing to the VNS. The VNS virtualizes and controls access to all IP network services, on a per micro-VM basis. Each micro-VM is assigned an anonymous IP address, its connections are NAT-ted, and IP services including the DNS are under control of the Microvisor, which can enforce the use of encryption (SSL or host based VPN) where necessary (e.g., for access to high-value sites), block IP services that are not permitted, and manage authentication and access control on behalf of each task, including single sign on. Finally, the VNS manages security functions typically found on an enterprise network: including the proxy, firewall, and traffic introspection and logging.

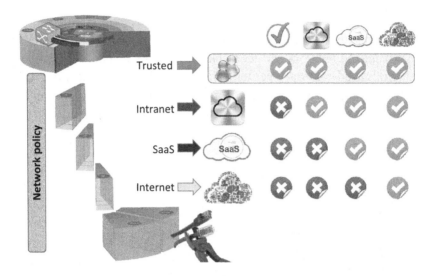

The Microvisor enforces granular isolation and privacy on a per-TLD basis. This offers each application (e.g., browser tab, or document) a defensible microperimeter by enforcing least privilege for access to all networks or sites. The mobile SDN hardware isolates, individually virtualizes, and controls all network services independently for each micro-VM, permitting granular policy controls on a per site basis. To understand the power of this capability we provide a detailed example as follows:

The user attaches their PC to the enterprise LAN and visits Facebook.com. The browser tab for Facebook.com will be invisibly isolated in a micro-VM, and by the rules of least privilege it will be granted access to only a single local file – the cookie for Facebook.com. What of its network services? Least privilege demands that the task for Facebook.com should:

- never be allowed to find or query the enterprise DNS, or access any intranet sites,
- never be allowed to resolve or access any high-value enterprise cloud/SaaS sites, such as Salesforce.com or AWS.Amazon.com,
- never be able to resolve or access the user's high-value sites (if configured) – such as their bank,
- never be able to find or communicate with any other application or micro-VM on the device, any devices on the LAN (including

printers), or any other enterprise application or infrastructure service or components – including the proxy, routers, switches or security appliances, networked file shares, and so forth.

- When attached to the LAN, the host manages all authentications, including NTLM authentication to proxies and shares, so that untrusted micro-VMs never have access to credentials.

These networking controls implement least privilege and give the browser tab for Facebook.com the privileges as an application running in the DMZ. If malware compromises the micro-VM, it can only access the untrusted internet.

5.10 VIRTUALIZED DESKTOP SERVICES

Micro-VMs access the user desktop via a virtual desktop service (VDS). The VDS provides an interface that does the following.

- Enables a micro-VM to deliver a 2-D display frame buffer to the host for compositing into the desktop user interface, and to deliver audio for delivery to host-controlled speakers. With increasing hardware capabilities, including virtualization-safe GPUs, it will shortly be possible to permit the micro-VM to directly render into its own hardware-isolated virtual GPU and portion of the frame-buffer, considerably accelerating graphics support and smoothly permitting a transition to 4K displays.
- Enforces printer redirection to allow the user to print an untrusted document, and
- Offers a virtual clipboard with modified semantics that prevent programmatic access – the user is required to interact with the system to complete any copy/paste action.

Whenever any information is passed to the VDS from a micro-VM, it is always flattened to ensure that the content does not contain latent executable code that could compromise the VDS or the host operating system.

In addition, the VDS manages user interaction with application menus (e.g., clicking "File/Save As" in a word document that is rendered in a micro-VM invokes a workflow that manages the export of an un-trusted file from a micro-VM to the host. The system therefore requires an understanding of application menu structure for all applications that are expected to run in a micro-VM. This is achieved through an XML annotation for each such application. Bromium Labs envisages such annotations becoming standard in application virtualization environments in the near future.[17]

5.11 CREATION AND MANAGEMENT OF MICRO-VMS

In a traditional hypervisor, virtualization-management tools are used to manage the lifecycle of VM instances. By contrast, because micro-VMs are application tasks run by the OS in response to user-initiated workflows, the lifecycle and resource management for micro-VMs needs to be fully integrated into the user experience of the device OS. This is a key requirement, since it permits us to use virtualization to deliver enhanced security and resilience without modifying the end-user experience.

Users should never be aware of the technology. Fortunately, integrating control into today's OSes is straightforward, for example, utilizing standard MIME-type handling interfaces. Each micro-VM is small when created (a few tens of MB), and grows over time on the basis of CoW differences between its state and the state of the golden host operating system – in both kernel and user mode. Most micro-VMs are short lived, but the system must remain fully functional even in the presence of long-running tasks that become large. To ensure consistent system performance under load, the Microvisor relies on the scheduler of the host OS, but occasionally enforces its own resource optimizations, optionally forcing micro-VMs to swap to disk (if idle) and pinning commonly accessed pages used by multiple micro-VMs in memory.

5.12 REDUCING THE ATTACK SURFACE

Many use cases of micro-virtualization are security or trust related. It is therefore important to understand the vulnerability of the Microvisor, since compromise of the Microvisor would make it possible for an attacker to attempt to compromise Windows.

---

[17] Wikipedia, "Microsoft Application Virtualization"

The Microvisor attack surface is narrow. Any access to system services outside the micro-VM (such as the file system or network services) occurs via enlightened service APIs. The enlightened services are simply DLL calls triggering a CPU VM_EXIT that allows the Microvisor to enforce access policies for the task. The Microvisor does not trust calls to this API (which is called the hypercall API), and the interface is resilient to attack and checkable by third parties. The Microvisor implements the hypercall API in about 10,000 lines of hardened code.

In summary, the Microvisor implements a Least Privilege Separation Kernel[18] between untrusted tasks and the desktop OS. It is the only Separation Kernel that takes advantage of the tiny code base of a specialized hypervisor to dynamically apply Least Privilege at a granular level between tasks within a single running OS instance. Moreover, it is the first general purpose Separation Kernel that can protect existing, widely deployed OSes and their applications, and that can be deployed and managed using today's management tools (Microsoft System Center, Active Directory, or a security management console).

---

[18] T. E. Levin, C. E. Irvine and T. D. Nguyen, "Least Privilege in Separation Kernels," in Security and Cryptography - SECRYPT, 2006.

CHAPTER 6

Advanced Forensics and Analysis

Bromium's Live Attack Visualization and Analysis (LAVA) uses the Microvisor to detect attacks and to provide powerful in-depth analysis of the behavior of advanced malware, before signatures are available. It also offers a powerful platform for forensic analysis that equips IT with vital information needed to understand the origin, targets, and vectors of an attack. With its multitier introspection framework, the centralized security application captures all the volatile information involved in the malware execution flow including the persistence aspects of the malware. This multipronged approach helps to notify users and IT reliably of compromised isolated tasks. The security operations teams can leverage this rich forensics information to act and tune their environments to limit the scope of further similar attacks.

The technology aims to identify attackers with a very high degree of accuracy, and to provide evidence of a compromise as soon as it occurs. There are three key advantages of the architecture that provide an opportunity for uniquely accurate and valuable detection and analysis:

- Courtesy of its privileged execution, the Microvisor has a unique perspective for introspection into a running micro-VM.
- Because a micro-VM is a restricted environment containing only one task, it is possible to easily detect behaviors that are anomalous for that task. Moreover, since micro-VMs execute Copy on Write, all changes made by any specific task are cached in its execution context, making it easy to associate attempted system changes with the specific task.
- Because the protect-first architecture will protect the system from an attack, malware need not be terminated early. Indeed, the attempted system modifications/compromises made by a task can be analyzed automatically when the task completes (or is closed by the user). Post-exploitation analysis of this form is dramatically simpler than pre-attack detection.

LAVA offers IT an ability to detect and study isolated malware to ascertain details about an attacker, his targets and methods, and to derive information to permit defense-in-depth.

6.1 Micro-VM BEHAVIORAL ANALYSIS

LAVA includes a powerful behavioral analysis engine. This engine operates with a malware detection approach that is highly tuned to deliver accurate identification of real attacks; in other words, few to no "False Positives." The engine combines insight into application/task layer semantics, with the narrow constraints of a microvirtualized execution environment.

The goal of the engine expressed in terms of the ROC diagram is shown below:

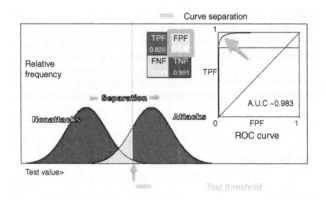

There are three key goals:

1. Provide a powerful new set of capabilities to separate attack and nonattack behavior as widely as possible, maximizing the ability of the detector to separate attack and nonattack events
2. Tune the detector to minimize False Positives (FPF ~ 0 due to the high threshold), and
3. Maximize True Positives.

6.2 ADVANCED LIVE FORENSICS

Every advanced attack typically follows a sequence:

The APT life cycle

Exploit	Execute	Escalate	Persist	Propagate
ROP shellcode	Dropper	Overwrite token	Modify registry	Reconnaissance
DLL injection	Download files	Get SYSTEM	Disable firewall	Infiltration

Systems that rely on detection in order to block an attack are heavily focused on the first two stages. They focus on this aspect because the moment an attacker has persisted an attack, the system is compromised and must be reimaged.

LAVA has an opportunity to permit malware to execute to completion without any fear of a succeeding attack. The attacker in a micro-VM will attempt to retain an attack by dropping a payload into the system in some way, and then will execute the attack. Since this solution manages persistence explicitly, any attempt to persist state will be detected. Further, since it has a powerful ability to introspect granular task-isolated micro-VMs, it gains unique insights that are not possible on any other computer system. For example, if an advanced BIOS-kit or bootkit tries to overwrite the MBR record to survive a reboot after compromising a task micro-VM, then the LAVA enabled Microvisor identifies this activity and alerts the administrator.

6.3 LAVA ARCHITECTURE

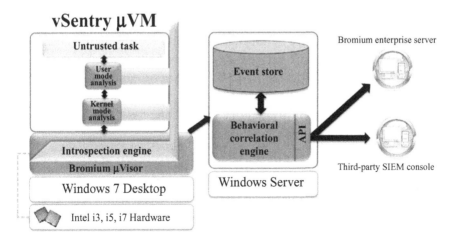

LAVA offers a set of powerful virtualization-enabled features that provide unparalleled insights into the behavior of new attacks, helping IT to identify attackers, their methods and targets, and enabling defense in depth through the use of complementary security tools. In particular, it offers a unique ability to tune the detection capability to "alert and block early" versus providing full late-stage, guaranteed malicious full forensics, via a simple tool that allows IT to select the optimum value.

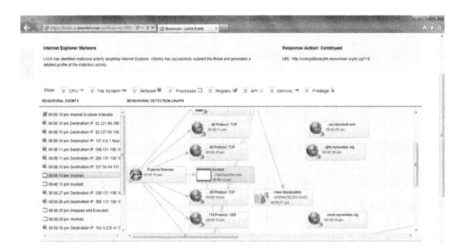

If desired, IT can study the behavior of the attacker in detail, observing its network traffic, changes that it attempts to make to the operating system and/or file system, and gain insight into the specific vulnerabilities it is using to execute the attack. Since the specific context in which the attack arrived at the desktop is available, together with the task state for the micro-VM, the forensic capability enables IT to pinpoint the origin of the attack and its vector into the enterprise. It also helps IT security to identify the specific assets targeted by the attacker.

The outputs of this solution are the entire forensic kill-chain, together with a captive malware manifest, in an open-industry standard format: STIX/MAEC that has been adopted by MITRE and federal agencies, the financial services industry and others. Events are output in real time, and are centralized at the Management Server where they can be delivered to various operations systems:

- Simple use of a tool such as Splunk> allows the C&C centers of an attack to be mapped in real time, as the attack occurs.
- The STIX forensic information can be parsed using Microsoft® Systems Center management workflows to trigger automated compliance checks and to force the user endpoint to be reexamined for security
- The output can be delivered to a SIEM or other vendor console
- The output can be delivered to a cloud-hosted "threat service" such as Microsoft MAPP, which can correlate malicious activity worldwide.

6.4 CONCLUSION

Attackers continue to increase the sophistication of their exploit techniques. Web browser release cycles are decreasing and the interval between the general availability of a new release and the appearance of the first security patches has also shortened. This may represent greater efforts on the part of software manufacturers to secure their products, or it may represent products being released to market with less security testing than earlier versions received. Notably "use-after-free" type vulnerabilities, zero-day attackers favorite.

The evolution from software-centric to hardware-based protection promises a revolution in on-line security and it heralds some unforeseen benefits: Although computers cannot discern good from bad, they are very good at enforcing the rules of "need to know" – even when we humans make mistakes. Appropriately implemented, such a system will protect the user by design when he/she mistakenly opens a malicious PDF document, or clicks on a poisoned URL.

Micro-virtualization extends the isolation, control, and isolation principles of hypervisor-based virtualization into the OS and its applications. It does this by using hardware virtualization to dynamically virtualize and isolate vulnerable user tasks. It provides a powerful, hardware-guaranteed backstop for the existing software isolation used in the OS, protecting sensitive applications and data, and allowing users to safely access untrusted networks, documents, and removable media. It is the only technology that can safely permit code and data of different levels of trust to coexist on a single system with guaranteed mutual isolation.

Micro-virtualization protects desktops from attack: Vulnerable tasks are isolated within the hardware-protected confines of a micro-VM. Micro-VMs execute with the full richness of Windows, but cannot modify the running desktop OS or applications; nor can they access privileged enterprise files, networks, web-sites, or devices. Any attempt by a micro-VM to access the file system, clipboard, network services, or any devices results in a hardware-forced VM_EXIT that returns control to the Microvisor that polices access to system resources – enforcing dynamic least-privilege access with mandatory access controls.

Micro-virtualization protects the desktop first and foremost, by preventing any micro-VM from tampering with Windows, gaining access to protected enterprise documents or data, or retaining an attack for later execution.

Micro-virtualization isolates individual user tasks into micro-VMs, offering security teams a powerful new vantage point from which to obtain real-time, automated analysis of malware attacks, without any concern that an attack might succeed. The granular isolation protects the desktop first and foremost, and also offers a secure, safe environment in which malware can be observed as it attempts to attack the enterprise.

When a new attack is identified, the incident response team can:

1. be confident that the attack has been isolated and hence defeated.
2. obtain detailed insight into how the attack was initiated, its targets and multiple vectors,
3. avoid the cost and downtime of remediation, because the architecture naturally discards malware, keeping systems "gold" and keeping users productive.

Any system that relies on on-the-fly detection of an attack in order to trigger protective measures – in other words the current state of the art in endpoint protection – faces a daunting task. Unfortunately no detector is perfect, and therefore an approach that depends on detection in order to protect is vulnerable to false negatives (i.e., failure to detect a real attack). If the attacker can bypass the detector, he will succeed. It is therefore imperative to adopt an approach that guarantees protection first and foremost, independent of any form of detection or analysis. The only system architecture that can deliver robust protection independent of any detection capability is micro-virtualization.

Printed in the United States
By Bookmasters